delights

afternoon delights

COFFEEHOUSE FAVORITES: *Cookies & Coffee Cake, Brownies & Bars, Scones & More*

JAMES McNAIR & ANDREW MOORE

photographs by KARL PETZKE / illustrations by DIANE BIGDA

CHRONICLE BOOKS
SAN FRANCISCO

Text copyright © 2001 by JAMES McNAIR and ANDREW MOORE.
Photographs copyright © 2001 by KARL PETZKE.
Illustrations copyright © 2001 by DIANE BIGDA.

Library of Congress Cataloging-in-Publication Data:

McNair, James K.

Afternoon delights : coffeehouse favorites, cookies and coffee cake,
brownies and bars, scones and more / by James McNair and Andrew Moore.
p. cm.
Includes index.
ISBN 0-8118-2996-0
1. Desserts. I. Moore, Andrew. II. Title
TX773 .M345 2001
641.8'6-dc21   00-065737

Designed by **VIVIEN SUNG**
Food styling by **DAN BECKER**

The photographer would like to thank the Vandine family for the use
of their beautiful home, Dan Becker for his wonderful and inspired food
styling, and his parents for requiring that he shoot only black & white
film in his first camera at age four.

Printed in China.

Distributed in Canada by Raincoast Books
9050 Shaughnessy Street
Vancouver, BC V6P 6E5

10 9 8 7 6 5 4 3 2 1

Chronicle Books LLC
85 Second Street
San Francisco, California 94105

www.chroniclebooks.com

dedication

For our great friends Michele Sordi *and* Pamela Davis*, who are delights at any time of day!*

And in memory of Joshua J. Chew*, the beloved golden retriever that we shared with our dear friend* John Carr*. A very special companion,* Josh *joined us in countless delightful afternoons catching tennis balls, swimming in Lake Tahoe, napping at our feet, and running free in High Sierra meadows. He left us on his fifteenth birthday, the same day that we signed the contract to write this book.*

acknowledgments

To Bill LeBlond, our editor, for letting us share our love of baking, and Amy Treadwell, his assistant, for keeping this book on schedule.

To Sharon Silva, our copyeditor, for her enthusiastic guidance and great work on our manuscript.

To Karen Mitchell for letting us have our portrait taken in her popular Model Bakery on Main Street in St. Helena, California, and to her staff for providing the delicious coffee and treats in the photograph.

To our family, friends, and neighbors who share our "sweet tooths" and inspired this book. Special thanks to those who were eager to sample and evaluate our recipe tests, including Almut and Rolf Busch; John Carr and Richard Ridgeway; Deborah Denehy; Maile, Mark, and Malia Forbert; Carol Gallagher and John Oosterbaan; Naila and Harold Gallagher; Jeanne Hoffman and Bill Moore; Jane Lidz and Bill Johnson; Marian May and Louis Hicks; Mary Val McCoy; Lucille McNair; Martha and Devereux McNair and John and Ryan Richardson; Sandy, Jim, Daniel, and Timmy Moore; Richard and Erin Moore; Gale and Hank Olson; Sara Moore and Masi, Kaeo, and Lyle Timpson; Terri, Mike, Bailey, and Kelsey Ryan; Ann and Efren Santos-Cucalon; and Marcie and Gregory Stapp.

To our furry family, Beauregard Ezekiel Valentine, Vivien Fleigh, Olivia de Puss Puss, and Michael T. Wigglebutt, who kept our kitchen cozy while we baked and were ever hopeful for any crumbs.

contents

Many of us look forward to a midafternoon pick-me-up.

It is the time of day when our energy flags and our stomachs rumble, and what we want is a familiar beverage and a sweet treat. So, for that needed lift, we often stop by the coffeehouses, espresso wagons, and boutique bakeries with coffee bars that dot our neighborhoods, downtowns, and shopping malls from coast to coast. And along with an afternoon espresso, latte, chai, or icy blended mocha, we indulge in a crisp cookie, gooey brownie, crumbly shortbread, or other treat to complement our steaming hot or frosty beverage. These afternoon delights bring sweet satisfaction.

We have spent many hours sampling the tantalizing treats on display at these emporiums. But as good as many commercially prepared versions may be, we know that such sweets are even better when freshly baked with a loving touch in a home kitchen.

We both were lucky to grow up in homes where the preparation and enjoyment of baked treats were welcomed family activities. James's earliest childhood cooking memories are of baking after-school snacks in the cozy kitchen of the Baptist parsonage in Jonesville, Louisiana, where he grew up. Before his mother and grandmothers taught him how to bake, he had limited his cooking to the creation of singular delicacies from the mud along the nearby levee. But by the time he was a teenager, James was an accomplished baker, and he spent countless hours whipping up scrumptious sweets for his family and for church events.

Andrew comes from a long line of good home bakers in Hawaii. His Gramma Bo was famous on Maui for her beautiful and delectable cakes, which she made a hobby of creating for birthdays, weddings, and other social gatherings. She passed on her love of baking to her children, including Andrew's mother, who enjoyed making festive cakes, cookies, and other treats and always had home-baked goodies on hand for Andrew and his four siblings in their Honolulu kitchen. Andrew's mother and her younger sister, his Auntie Naila (who "adopted" him after his mother passed away), were happy to teach and share the "joy of baking" with him as he grew up.

Our childhood cooking interests have since grown into food-related careers, and along with producing cookbooks on a wide variety of subjects, we continue the pleasurable pursuit of good home baking. We especially enjoy making cookies, brownies, and other similar small treats, and like to put them out when we get together for afternoon coffee or tea with friends and family members. Since our guests have often seemed amazed by the offerings from our kitchen and have repeatedly asked us for recipes, we have decided to do this little volume.

For this collection, we visited numerous coffee emporiums and chose popular afternoon treats regularly served by them.

We noticed that most contemporary establishments carry both American and European baked classics. That's because they know that sometimes our "grown-up" tastes want sophisticated biscotti, madeleines, and scones, while at other times the kids within us are nostalgic for homey oatmeal cookies, seven-layer bars, banana bread, and other comforting treats that we remember from our childhood.

After researching recipes and making countless versions of these popular offerings, we put together what we considered the finest elements from them and developed basic recipes and variations, along with a few new ideas of our own. As we wrote this book, we kept in mind both novice cooks and accomplished bakers and tried to create the very best recipes possible for the home kitchen. During numerous recipe tests, we took note of our baking techniques and summed up our findings in the tips that follow this introduction.

We hope that our recipes will become favorites in your home, and that they will indeed make your afternoons delightful.

13

ingredients bakeware preparing baking sheets and pans getting starte
storing yields ingredients bakeware preparing baking sheets and pan
chocolate serving storing yields ingredients bakeware preparing ba
cooling dipping in chocolate serving storing yields ingredients bal

TIPS FOR SWEET SUCCESS

measuring and mixing forming and baking cooling dipping in chocolate se
etting started measuring and mixing forming and baking cooling dipping
g sheets and pans getting started measuring and mixing forming and bakin
are preparing baking sheets and pans getting started measuring and mixing

To help make baking *afternoon delights* easier, foolproof, and more fun, here are some general guidelines for good baking, plus a few personal opinions and "pearls of wisdom." Also included are suggestions for serving and for adjusting recipe yields. Probably the most valuable tip that we can share is to remind you to read all the way through a recipe before starting it, to avoid any surprises!

ingredients

Any baked treat is only as good as its components, so always use the freshest and finest-quality ingredients.

Use unsalted butter, not only because we call for it and have given salt measurements accordingly, but because it also tends to be fresher than salted butter.

Unless bleached flour is specified, you may use either bleached or unbleached flour when a recipe calls for all-purpose flour. Bleached flour and Southern all-purpose flour, such as White Lily brand, have less protein than unbleached flour and yield more-tender treats. We use cake flour, which is very soft and low in protein, for delicate madeleines.

High-quality chocolate and chocolate chips are essential. You may already have favorite brands, or you might try several different ones to see which you prefer. We like "luxury" products, such as Sharffen Berger, Callebaut, and Valrhona. Be sure that the white chocolate you use contains cocoa butter.

When recipes call for nuts, be sure that they are fresh. In most cases, we toast them to bring out their rich flavor and make them extraspecial. To toast, spread the amount of shelled nuts specified in a recipe in a single layer in a baking pan. Transfer the pan to an oven that has been preheated to 350 degrees F, and toast the nuts, stirring occasionally, until lightly browned and fragrant, about 10 minutes. Remove the pan from the oven, pour the nuts onto a plate, and let cool completely before using in recipes.

| bakeware |

Insulated (two-layer) plain aluminum baking sheets (not dark, nonstick ones) are ideal for baking cookies and scones, as they prevent them from browning too quickly. For good heat circulation, a sheet should have at least 2 inches clearance from the oven walls on all sides, so measure your oven before you go shopping.

For brownies, bars, quick breads, and coffee cakes, heavy-duty aluminum pans with a dull finish work best for even baking. Dark pans, including nonstick ones, absorb heat too quickly and can overbrown the bottoms and edges of the baked goods before the centers are done.

| preparing baking
sheets and pans |

For easy removal of baked cookies and scones, we recommend lining baking sheets with kitchen parchment (sold in many supermarkets and cookware stores) or silicone baking mats (available from cookware stores, catalogs, or Web sites under such brand names as Exopat and Silpat). To line with kitchen parchment, use scissors to cut a piece the exact dimensions of the bottom of the baking sheet, and place it on the sheet. To line with a silicone baking mat, choose a mat of the same size as your baking sheet and place it on the sheet. A parchment lining can be reused several times: wipe off any crumbs between batches until it becomes too brittle or greasy for reuse. A silicone mat can be reused thousands of times: wipe it clean between batches and wash it after your baking is done for the day.

We like to use solid vegetable shortening such as Crisco for greasing pans for brownies, bars, and coffee cakes. It is flavorless and coats evenly. Use a pastry brush for greasing and be sure to coat every nook and cranny of the pan for easy and even removal. If you object to the use of hydrogenated shortening, you can coat pans with butter. Just keep in mind that butter melts at a lower temperature than solid shortening and, during baking, may melt and leave ungreased gaps to which baked goods can stick. Butter can also burn or cause the crust of baked goods to overbrown.

Some bakers line the pans for brownies or bars with aluminum foil that overhangs the edges of the pan. The baked sweet can then be lifted out in one piece and transferred to a cutting surface for easier slicing into bars or pieces. This method also allows you to trim off hard edges easily. To line a pan with foil, first grease the bottom and sides of the pan with vegetable shortening as described in the preceding paragraph. Cut two pieces of foil that are long enough and wide enough to fit inside the pan and overhang the edges when stacked perpendicular to each other. Place the foil pieces in the pan and smooth them with your fingers across the bottom and up the sides, then brush the bottom and sides with shortening.

For quick breads, we prefer not to flour loaf pans after greasing. Instead, we line the bottoms of the pans with kitchen parchment for easy release of the breads. With this method, less crust forms on the bottoms and sides of the loaves. To line a pan, place it on a piece of parchment and trace around the bottom with a pencil, then cut out the traced shape with scissors. Lay the parchment cutout on the bottom of the greased pan and use your fingers to smooth out any wrinkles.

| getting started |

Have all ingredients ready before you start working on a recipe. Certain ingredients take time to prepare, like toasted nuts or chopped chocolate, and you don't want to stop in the middle of mixing a batter to prepare them.

For better blending, butter and eggs, and sometimes milk products, are often specified to be at room temperature, which should be about 70 degrees F. Remove these items from the refrigerator an hour or so before starting a recipe, and set them in a warm spot (but not in direct sunlight).

If you forget to do this (or have a sudden urge to bake), you can warm eggs quickly by placing them in a bowl of warm water, and milk products can be swiftly heated in a microwave oven. Butter can also be warmed in a microwave oven: use low power and run the oven for only 5 or 10 seconds at a time until the butter is pliable but not overly soft. A microwave oven does a speedy job of melting butter as well. Use a heatproof glass measuring cup for easy pouring.

measuring and mixing

Baking is a science, so accuracy is important. Use metal or plastic measuring cups made specifically for dry ingredients. Measure flour and other dry ingredients, including leavenings and spices, using the "spoon-and-sweep" method: spoon the ingredient into a measuring cup or spoon of the proper size and fill it to overflowing, then use a knife or straight edge to sweep off the excess.

For liquid ingredients, use glass or plastic measuring cups made with pouring lips and measurement marks on the sides. Set the measuring cup on a level surface and pour in the liquid until it reaches the proper mark.

Most of our recipes call for using an electric mixer at some point. Use a heavy-duty mixer, so it won't overheat on stiff batters or doughs. A hand mixer will work fine for most tasks, but a stand mixer will free up your hands to make adding ingredients easier. When using an electric mixer, stop the machine occasionally during the mixing process and scrape the beater(s) and sides of the bowl to incorporate any mixture that may be clinging.

Unless directed otherwise, when adding flour or a flour mixture to batters or doughs, mix gently (or at low speed if using an electric mixer) just until it is incorporated. Overmixing will overdevelop the gluten in flour and make for tough treats instead of tender delights.

forming and baking

Even, accurate heat is essential for successful baking. It's a good idea to check your oven temperature periodically with an oven thermometer (available at most supermarkets) and adjust the oven dial if needed to achieve the temperature indicated in a recipe.

To form "drop cookies" of equal size that will all be done at the same time, use an ice-cream scoop with a release mechanism (also sold as a disher or a portion scoop). For each cookie, scoop up enough dough to fill the scoop to overflowing, then use a knife or straight edge to sweep off the excess dough. Turn out the level portion of dough onto the baking sheet, or roll the portion into a ball and place on the sheet as directed in some recipes.

Avoid crowding cookies on a baking sheet, as they need space around them for good heat circulation. Many cookies also need room to spread as they bake. In each recipe, we have specified the amount of space between cookies, allowing more generous spacing for those that spread.

All the baked goods in this book should be baked in the middle of an oven, where the heat is most even. Position an oven rack accordingly before preheating the oven. When baking, place the baking sheet or pan on the center of the rack for good heat circulation.

For the most consistent results in timing, appearance, and doneness, bake only one batch of cookies at a time and leave them alone during the baking process. We do not recommend rotating a baking sheet 180 degrees halfway through baking, nor do we suggest baking two batches at the same time on separate racks and switching their positions between the racks halfway through baking.

When baking, start checking for doneness, as described in each recipe, several minutes before the time we have specified. Every oven is different, and baked goods can go quickly from perfect to dry or burned.

| cooling | Use a heavy-duty wire rack for cooling sheets and pans. Unless directed otherwise, after a few minutes of cooling on the baking sheet to let them set up, cookies should be transferred directly to the rack to finish cooling, as the bottoms may overbrown if left on the hot sheet.

When baking another batch of cookies, don't place cookie dough on a hot baking sheet—it will start melting before going into the oven and the cookies will not bake evenly. If you are using the same baking sheet for each batch, after removing the cookies, slip off the parchment or baking mat and wipe it clean for reuse as previously described. Then rinse the sheet under cold running water to cool it quickly, dry it well, and line it again with the parchment or mat.

| dipping in chocolate | Biscotti (page 27), Coconut Macaroons (page 35), Peanut Butter Cookies (page 50), Shortbreads (page 43), and other cookies become decadent treats when dipped in chocolate. We usually dip cookies only partially into chocolate, so that their natural beauty isn't completely hidden and their flavor isn't overwhelmed. Round, flat cookies such as peanut butter cookies and long cookies such as biscotti and shortbreads are elegant when dipped halfway, while dipping only the bottoms of macaroons enhances their mounded shape.

To dip cookies, first line a baking sheet or tray that will fit in your refrigerator with kitchen parchment and set it alongside the cookies. For a dozen large cookies, coarsely chop 8 ounces best-quality chocolate and place it in a heatproof bowl. Set the bowl in a skillet or shallow saucepan containing about 1 inch of barely simmering water and stir the chocolate constantly just until melted and smooth; do not allow it to burn. Remove the bowl from the heat and set it between the cookies and lined sheet or tray. Working quickly, dip a cookie in the chocolate, hold it briefly over the bowl to catch any drips, then place it on the sheet or tray. Repeat with the remaining cookies. (If the chocolate becomes too hard for dipping, return the bowl to the simmering water and stir the chocolate constantly just until it is melted and smooth, then resume dipping.) Transfer the sheet or tray to the refrigerator and chill the cookies just until the chocolate is firm, about 30 minutes. Remove the cookies from the refrigerator and let come to room temperature before serving, or store as directed in recipes.

| serving |

We eat first with our eyes, so present your home-baked afternoon delights appealingly arranged on beautiful serving plates or trays.

If you line a pan with aluminum foil for brownies or bars, as described earlier, after baking and cooling, use the overhanging foil edges to lift the treat out of the pan in one piece and set it down on a baking sheet. Invert another baking sheet over the treat, invert the sheets together, lift off the top sheet, and peel off the foil. Then invert the treat again onto a cutting board, so that the top side is up, and cut as directed.

Since we usually don't line pans for brownies and bars with aluminum foil, we cut them, as well as coffee cakes, in their pans just before serving, using a heavy-duty, rigid plastic utensil to avoid scratching the pans. We then use a spatula to transfer them to a serving plate.

| storing |

All of the baked goods in this book can be stored at room temperature (a cool spot out of direct sunlight is best) except the lemon bars, which must be refrigerated after several hours. We have specified what we consider the best storage procedure and maximum storage time for each recipe. But most baked goods are best when eaten on the day they are made. Crisp cookies get soft, chewy cookies get hard, and moist brownies, bars, and coffee cakes dry out quickly no matter how airtight they are stored. Exceptions to the rule are quick breads, which actually taste and slice better the day after baking and keep for a week, and biscotti, Russian tea cakes, and shortbreads, which keep well for up to 2 weeks.

If you need to bake ahead, or wish to save leftovers, you may freeze scones, quick breads, and coffee cakes successfully for up to 1 month. After cooling completely, wrap quick breads and coffee cakes tightly in plastic wrap, then in aluminum foil, and freeze. Place scones in plastic freezer bags and freeze. Thaw them all in your refrigerator or at room temperature, and let them return to room temperature before serving. We do not recommend freezing cookies, brownies, and bars, however, as most of them become unappealingly sticky or crumbly after thawing.

yields

Our recipes are written to satisfy big sweet cravings, so they make large cookies, brownies, bars, and scones, and large slices of quick breads and coffee cakes, just as you would find served in most coffeehouses.

For less-hearty appetites, you may reduce the size of "drop cookies" by using smaller ice-cream scoops to form the dough. The cookies will be done a few minutes earlier than the specified baking times, and you will end up with more of them. A #40 (about 2-tablespoon) scoop should yield about twice as many cookies, each about half the size, and a #100 (about 1-tablespoon) scoop should yield about four times the original quantity and make even smaller cookies. To make smaller Linzer cookies, use cutters with smaller diameters. Biscotti and shortbread dough can be sliced into smaller cookies before baking. You may also make more and smaller scones by slicing the dough into more portions or by cutting out shapes with a biscuit or cookie cutter. And brownies, bars, quick breads, and coffee cakes may be easily cut or sliced into smaller portions.

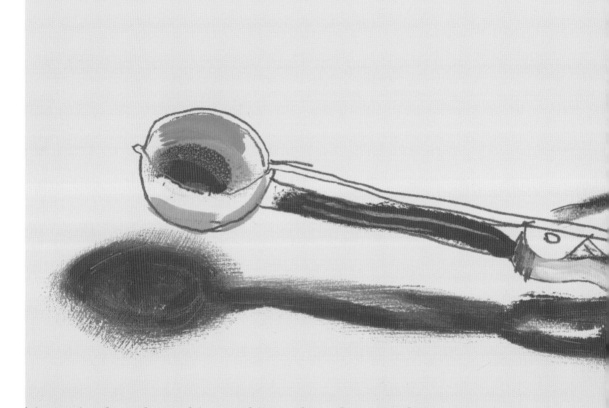

biscotti   chocolate chip cookies   chocolate mudpies   coconut macaroon
cookies   peanut butter cookies   snickerdoodles   linzer cookies   biscotti
madeleines   shortbreads   molasses ginger crinkles   oatmeal raisin cooki
cookies   chocolate mudpies   coconut macaroons   russian tea cakes   ma

COOKIES

ussian tea cakes madeleines shortbreads molasses ginger crinkles oatmeal r
ocolate chip cookies chocolate mudpies coconut macaroons russian tea cake
eanut butter cookies snickerdoodles linzer cookies biscotti chocolate chip
ines shortbreads molasses ginger crinkles oatmeal raisin cookies peanut bu

These long, sliced, twice-baked Italian cookies are coffeehouse classics. Our recipe yields biscotti that are dry and crunchy and not too sweet—perfect for dipping into hot coffee, espresso, or tea. The chocolate-dipped variation adds a nice touch to both the look and the flavor.

biscotti / *Makes about 1 dozen large biscotti*

2 cups all-purpose flour

1 cup granulated sugar

2 teaspoons baking powder

1/4 teaspoon salt

3 large eggs, lightly beaten

1 teaspoon pure almond extract (if using almonds) or
2 teaspoons pure vanilla extract (if using other nuts)

1 cup almonds, hazelnuts, pistachios, pine nuts,
or other nuts, lightly toasted (see page 16) and coarsely chopped

1. Position an oven rack so that the biscotti will bake in the middle of the oven and preheat the oven to 300 degrees F. Line a baking sheet with kitchen parchment or a silicone baking mat and set aside.

2. In a bowl, combine the flour, sugar, baking powder, and salt and whisk to mix well. Add the eggs and almond or vanilla extract and mix well with a spoon (the mixture will be crumbly). Stir in the toasted nuts.

3. Transfer the mixture to a lightly floured work surface. Dust your hands with flour and gently knead the dough until it comes together, about 1 minute (the dough will be sticky). Transfer the dough to the lined baking sheet. Using a ruler as a guide and dusting your hands with flour as needed, →

shape the dough into an even, flat rectangle about 6 by 9 inches.

4. Transfer the baking sheet to the oven and bake until the dough is lightly golden and feels firm when lightly touched in the center with your fingertip, about 50 minutes. (The dough will spread into a large, rounded rectangle as it bakes.)

5. Remove the baking sheet to a wire rack to cool for about 15 minutes, then peel the dough rectangle from the parchment or baking mat and transfer it to a cutting board. Wipe off any crumbs from the parchment or baking mat, return it to the baking sheet, and set aside. Using a serrated knife, first slice off and discard the rounded edges of the 2 shorter sides of the dough rectangle to make straight sides, then continue slicing the rectangle into slices about 3/4 inch wide. Lay the slices, with one of their cut sides down, about 1 inch apart on the lined baking sheet.

6. Return the baking sheet to the oven and bake until the exposed cut sides of the slices are golden, about 20 minutes. Then remove the sheet from the oven, turn the biscotti over, return the sheet to the oven, and con-

tinue baking until the other exposed sides of the biscotti are golden, about 20 minutes longer.

7. Remove the baking sheet to a wire rack to cool for a few minutes. When the biscotti are cool enough to handle, transfer them directly to the rack to cool completely.

The biscotti may be stored in an airtight container at room temperature for up to 2 weeks.

VARIATIONS

Chocolate Chip Biscotti *Substitute chocolate chips for the nuts. When slicing the dough, you will need to wipe the knife blade after each cut to remove melted chocolate.*

Chocolate-Dipped Biscotti *See page 21.*

Fruit Biscotti *Substitute dried currants, raisins, or coarsely chopped dried blueberries, cranberries, or sour cherries for the nuts.*

Ginger Biscotti *Substitute 1/2 cup coarsely chopped crystallized ginger for the nuts.*

Ever since Mrs. Wakefield stirred together the original batch of chocolate chip cookies at her Toll House Inn in 1930, they have been America's most popular cookie. Our chewy version has lots of toasted nuts for extra flavor. For a more sophisticated cookie, chop 6 ounces of premium semisweet chocolate and use in place of the chips. The white chocolate and macadamia nut variation is another coffeehouse favorite.

chocolate
chip cookies / *Makes about 1 dozen large cookies*

1¹/4 cups all-purpose flour
¹/2 teaspoon baking soda
¹/2 teaspoon salt
¹/2 cup (1 stick) unsalted butter, at room temperature
¹/2 cup granulated sugar
¹/2 cup firmly packed light brown sugar
1 large egg, at room temperature
2 teaspoons pure vanilla extract
1 cup semisweet chocolate chips
1 cup pecans or walnuts, lightly toasted (see page 16) and coarsely chopped

1. Position an oven rack so that the cookies will bake in the middle of the oven and preheat the oven to 350 degrees F. Line a baking sheet with kitchen parchment or a silicone baking mat and set aside.

2. In a bowl, combine the flour, baking soda, and salt. Whisk to mix well and set aside.

3. In another bowl, combine the butter and sugars and beat with an electric mixer at medium speed until the mixture is light and fluffy, about 5 minutes. Add the egg and vanilla and blend well. Add the flour mixture and mix at low speed just until incorporated. Stir in the chocolate chips and toasted nuts. →

4. Using a #20 ($1/4$-cup) ice-cream scoop, scoop up level portions of the dough and place them about 3 inches apart on the lined baking sheet until the sheet is full. (Cover the remaining dough tightly with plastic wrap to prevent drying out and set aside until forming the next batch of cookies.)

5. Transfer the baking sheet to the oven and bake until the cookies are golden brown, about 15 minutes.

6. Remove the baking sheet to a wire rack to cool for a few minutes, then using a spatula, transfer the cookies directly to the rack to cool completely.

7. Repeat the forming and baking process until the dough is used up.

The cookies may be stored in an airtight container at room temperature for up to 3 days.

VARIATION

White Chocolate and Macadamia Nut Cookies *Substitute 6 ounces white chocolate, coarsely chopped, or 1 cup white chocolate chips for the semisweet chocolate chips. Substitute macadamia nuts for the pecans or walnuts.*

Most coffeehouses have some version of a fudgy chocolate "cookie" that's almost a brownie. Our recipe makes rich, dense treats that look like childhood mudpies. Almonds or macadamia nuts can be used in place of the pecans or walnuts. Mocha Mudpies, which combine coffee and chocolate, make a divine variation.

chocolate
mudpies / *Makes about 1 dozen large cookies*

1/4 cup bleached all-purpose flour

1/4 teaspoon baking powder

1/8 teaspoon salt

1 pound semisweet chocolate, coarsely chopped

2 tablespoons unsalted butter, cut into small pieces

1/2 cup granulated sugar

2 large eggs, at room temperature

1 teaspoon pure vanilla extract

1 cup pecans or walnuts, lightly toasted (see page 16) and coarsely chopped

1. In a bowl, combine the flour, baking powder, and salt. Whisk to mix well and set aside.

2. In a small stainless-steel bowl, combine half of the chopped chocolate with the butter. Set the bowl in a skillet or shallow saucepan containing about 1 inch of barely simmering water and stir the chocolate mixture gently until melted and smooth.

Remove the bowl from the heat and set aside to cool slightly.

3. In a bowl, combine the sugar and eggs and beat with an electric mixer at high speed until the mixture is thick and pale yellow, about 5 minutes. Add the melted chocolate mixture and vanilla and blend well. Add the flour mixture and mix at low speed just

until incorporated. Stir in the remaining chopped chocolate and the toasted nuts. Cover the bowl tightly with plastic wrap and refrigerate until the dough is firm enough to handle, about 30 minutes.

4. Position an oven rack so that the cookies will bake in the middle of the oven and preheat the oven to 350 degrees F. Line a baking sheet with kitchen parchment or a silicone baking mat.

5. Using a #20 (1/4-cup) ice-cream scoop, scoop up level portions of dough and place them about 3 inches apart on the lined baking sheet until the sheet is full. (Cover the remaining dough tightly with plastic wrap to prevent drying out and refrigerate until forming the next batch of cookies.) Press down on the dough portions with your fingertips to form each portion into a rough round about 1/2 inch thick.

6. Transfer the baking sheet to the oven and bake until the tops of the cookies feel just set when lightly touched with your fingertip, about 10 minutes.

7. Remove the baking sheet to a wire rack to cool for about 10 minutes, then using a spatula, transfer the cookies directly to the rack to cool completely.

8. Repeat the forming and baking process until the dough is used up.

The cookies may be stored in an airtight container at room temperature for up to 3 days.

VARIATION

Mocha Mudpies *Add 1/4 cup instant espresso powder, preferably Medaglia d'Oro brand (available in Italian grocery stores and upscale supermarkets), to the melted chocolate-butter mixture after removing from the heat and stir until dissolved.*

We are coconut addicts, and these large macaroons, with their crunchy, toasted exteriors and gooey, chewy interiors, bring swift satisfaction to our cravings. When we dip the bottoms in melted bittersweet chocolate, we ascend to coconut heaven!

coconut
macaroons / *Makes about 1 dozen large cookies*

2 packages (7 ounces each) sweetened shredded coconut (about 4 cups)

1¹/2 cups granulated sugar

1 cup egg whites (from about 8 large eggs)

¹/2 cup all-purpose flour

2 teaspoons pure vanilla extract

¹/4 teaspoon salt

1. Position an oven rack so that the cookies will bake in the middle of the oven and pre-heat the oven to 350 degrees F. Line a baking sheet with kitchen parchment or a silicone baking mat and set aside.

2. In a heavy saucepan, combine all of the ingredients and mix thoroughly. Place over medium heat and cook, stirring constantly and scraping the bottom of the pan to prevent scorching, until the mixture is fairly dry and stiff, about 10 minutes. Remove from the heat.

3. Using a #20 (¹/4-cup) ice-cream scoop, scoop up level portions of the mixture and place them about 1 inch apart on the lined baking sheet.

4. Transfer the baking sheet to the oven and bake until the macaroons are golden brown, about 20 minutes.

5. Remove the baking sheet to a wire rack to cool for about 5 minutes, then peel the macaroons from the parchment or baking mat, place them directly on the rack, and let cool completely.

The macaroons may be stored in an airtight container at room temperature for up to 3 days.

VARIATION

Chocolate-Dipped Coconut Macaroons *See page 21.*

When made with pecans, our nut of choice, these light-as-air cookies are known as Mexican or Portuguese wedding cakes. Almonds are used to make the Greek version, *kourabiedes*. By any name and made with whichever nuts, the powdered sugar–dusted buttery cookies are one of our favorites for serving with afternoon tea.

russian
tea cakes / *Makes about 1 dozen large cookies*

1½ cups walnuts or other nuts (see recipe introduction), lightly toasted (see page 16)
⅓ cup granulated sugar
2 cups bleached all-purpose flour
½ teaspoon salt
1 cup (2 sticks) unsalted butter, at room temperature
2 teaspoons pure vanilla extract
Powdered sugar for dusting

1. In a food processor, combine the toasted nuts and the granulated sugar and process until the nuts are very finely ground. Add the flour and salt, pulse to blend well, and set aside.

2. In a bowl, beat the butter with an electric mixer at medium speed until light and fluffy, about 3 minutes. Add the vanilla and beat well. Add the nut-flour mixture and mix at medium speed until combined and the mixture holds together, about 2 minutes. Cover the bowl tightly with plastic wrap and refrigerate until the dough is well chilled, at least 2 hours.

3. Position an oven rack so that the cookies will bake in the middle of the oven and preheat the oven to 325 degrees F. Line a baking sheet with kitchen parchment or a silicone baking mat and set aside. →

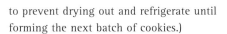

4. Using a #20 ($1/4$-cup) ice-cream scoop, scoop up level portions of the dough and place them about 3 inches apart on the lined baking sheet until the sheet is full. (Cover the remaining dough tightly with plastic wrap to prevent drying out and refrigerate until forming the next batch of cookies.)

5. Transfer the baking sheet to the oven and bake until the cookies are golden brown around the edges, about 25 minutes.

6. Remove the baking sheet to a wire rack to cool for about 10 minutes, then using a spatula, transfer the cookies directly to the rack. Sift a generous amount of powdered sugar over each cookie to coat completely and let the cookies cool completely.

7. Repeat the forming, baking, and coating process until the dough is used up.

The cookies may be stored in an airtight container at room temperature for up to 2 weeks.

Eloquently praised in the work of the French novelist Marcel Proust, these old-fashioned treats are popular in twenty-first-century coffeehouses and tea shops. Although spongy, dry madeleines are technically little cakes, they are traditionally dipped into coffee or tea and eaten like cookies.

madeleines / *Makes about 2 dozen madeleines*

3/4 cup (1 1/2 sticks) unsalted butter

1 cup cake flour

3 large eggs

1 large egg yolk

2/3 cup granulated sugar

1/4 teaspoon salt

1 teaspoon finely grated or minced fresh lemon zest

1 1/2 teaspoons pure vanilla extract

Solid vegetable shortening, at room temperature, for greasing

All-purpose flour for dusting

Powdered sugar for dusting

1. In a small, heavy saucepan, place the butter over medium heat and heat until the milk solids separate, drop to the bottom of the pan, and turn a rich brown; do not allow to burn. Remove from the heat and set aside.

2. Place the cake flour in a strainer or sifter, sift into a bowl, and set aside.

3. In a bowl, combine the eggs, egg yolk, granulated sugar, and salt and beat with an electric mixer at high speed until very pale and creamy, about 5 minutes. Add half of the cake flour and mix at low speed until well blended. Mix in the browned butter in the same manner, then blend in the remaining →

just below the rims. Alternatively, transfer the chilled batter to a pastry bag fitted with a coupler and pipe the batter into the molds, again filling to just below the rims. (Cover the remaining batter tightly with plastic wrap to prevent drying out and set aside until forming the next batch of madeleines.)

6. Transfer the pan to the oven and bake until the tops of the madeleines are golden and spring back when lightly touched in their centers with your fingertip, 8 to 10 minutes.

7. Remove the pan from the oven and immediately turn out the madeleines, shell sides up, onto a wire rack to cool completely.

8. Wash and dry the pan, then fill and bake again as directed.

The madeleines may be stored in an airtight container at room temperature for up to 3 days. Just before serving, sift a light dusting of powdered sugar over them.

flour. Add the lemon zest and vanilla and mix until smooth. Cover the bowl tightly with plastic wrap and refrigerate for about 30 minutes.

4. Position an oven rack so that the madeleines will bake in the middle of the oven and preheat the oven to 375 degrees F. Using a pastry brush, generously grease the 12 scallop shell-shaped molds of a madeleine pan (available from cookware stores, catalogs, or Web sites) with shortening. Sprinkle the greased molds generously with all-purpose flour, tilt and rotate the pan to coat the molds evenly, invert the pan over a sink, and tap the bottom to remove excess flour. Set aside.

5. Spoon a generous tablespoon of the batter into each of the prepared molds, filling to

The name *shortbread* refers to the high ratio of shortening, actually butter, to flour that results in these exceptionally tender and crumbly treats. To some of us, a shortbread, with its simple, pure flavor, is the perfect cookie. We prefer to bake shortbreads as individual cookies rather than in a single sheet, to be cut after baking into bars or wedges, as they get crispier and the edges get nicely browned.

shortbreads / *Makes 1 dozen large cookies*

1½ cups (3 sticks) unsalted butter, at room temperature
3/4 cup granulated sugar
1/4 teaspoon salt
2 teaspoons pure vanilla extract
3 cups bleached all-purpose flour

1. Using a ruler and pencil, draw an 8-by-12-inch rectangle on a piece of kitchen parchment. Place the parchment on a lightweight cutting board that will fit in your refrigerator. Set aside.

2. In a bowl, beat the butter with an electric mixer at medium speed until soft and creamy, about 45 seconds. Add the sugar and salt and mix until well blended. Add the vanilla and blend well. Add the flour, about 1 cup at a time, and mix until the dough is smooth, about 2 minutes.

3. Scrape the dough onto the parchment, placing it within the boundaries of the drawn rectangle. Place a piece of plastic wrap over the dough. Using your fingertips, press out the dough through the plastic wrap to make an even rectangle with a smooth surface and straight edges that fit the drawn rectangle. Press the plastic wrap gently onto the dough →

6. Transfer the baking sheet to the oven and bake until the tops of the shortbreads are pale golden all over, about 45 minutes. The edges will be lightly browned, but do not allow the tops to brown.

7. Remove the baking sheet to a wire rack to cool completely.

8. Repeat the baking process until the shortbreads are all baked.

The shortbreads may be stored in an airtight container at room temperature for up to 2 weeks.

VARIATION

Chocolate-Dipped Shortbreads
See page 21.

to seal it in. Refrigerate the dough on the cutting board until well chilled, at least 2 hours.

4. Position an oven rack so that the shortbreads will bake in the middle of the oven and preheat the oven to 300 degrees F. Line a baking sheet with kitchen parchment or a silicone baking mat.

5. Remove the chilled dough from the refrigerator and remove the plastic wrap. Using a ruler as a guide, quickly slice the dough with a sharp knife into 2-by-4-inch pieces to form 12 rectangles. Place the rectangles about 2 inches apart on the lined baking sheet, until the sheet is full. (Cover and refrigerate the remaining dough until baking the next batch.)

Spicy and sweet, these are the perfect winter-time treat. Rolling the dough balls in sugar gives the cookies extra crunch, and using raw sugar for coating boosts the molasses flavor.

molasses
ginger crinkles / *Makes about 1 dozen large cookies*

About 1/4 cup large sugar crystals, raw sugar, or granulated sugar for
   rolling (see recipe introduction)
2 cups all-purpose flour
1 teaspoon baking soda
1/2 teaspoon salt
2 teaspoons ground ginger
1 teaspoon ground cinnamon
1/2 teaspoon ground cloves
1/2 cup (1 stick) unsalted butter, at room temperature
1 cup granulated sugar
1/4 cup light molasses
1 large egg, at room temperature

1. Position an oven rack so that the cookies will bake in the middle of the oven and preheat the oven to 350 degrees F. Line a baking sheet with kitchen parchment or a silicone baking mat and set aside. Place 1/4 cup of the selected sugar for rolling in a shallow bowl and set aside.

2. In a bowl, combine the flour, baking soda, salt, ginger, cinnamon, and cloves. Whisk to mix well and set aside.

3. In another bowl, combine the butter and the 1 cup granulated sugar and beat with an electric mixer at medium speed until the mixture is light and fluffy, about 5 minutes. Add the molasses and egg and blend well. Add the flour mixture, about 1 cup at a time, and mix at low speed just until incorporated.

4. Using a #20 (1/4-cup) ice-cream scoop, scoop up a level portion of dough. Roll the dough portion between your palms to form a →

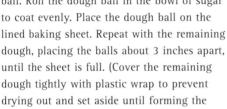

ball. Roll the dough ball in the bowl of sugar to coat evenly. Place the dough ball on the lined baking sheet. Repeat with the remaining dough, placing the balls about 3 inches apart, until the sheet is full. (Cover the remaining dough tightly with plastic wrap to prevent drying out and set aside until forming the

next batch of cookies.) Press down on the dough balls with your fingertips to form each ball into a round about 1/2 inch thick.

5. Transfer the baking sheet to the oven and bake until the cookies are lightly browned, about 15 minutes.

6. Remove the baking sheet to a wire rack to cool for a few minutes, then using a spatula, transfer the cookies directly to the rack to cool completely.

7. Repeat the forming and baking process until the dough is used up. Refill the bowl of sugar for rolling if needed.

The cookies may be stored in an airtight container at room temperature for up to 3 days.

As cozy as a country kitchen, oatmeal cookies are an American classic—the traditional "comfort cookies." Our version uses lots of old-fashioned rolled oats for maximum chewiness. Although typically made with raisins, dried cranberries or blueberries or chopped dried sour cherries can be used instead, or see the variations that follow for other wonderful additions.

oatmeal
raisin cookies / *Makes about 1 dozen large cookies*

1/2 cup all-purpose flour

1/2 teaspoon baking soda

1/2 teaspoon salt

3/4 cup (11/2 sticks) unsalted butter, at room temperature

1 cup firmly packed light brown sugar

1/2 cup granulated sugar

1 large egg, at room temperature

2 teaspoons pure vanilla extract

3 cups old-fashioned (not quick-cooking) rolled oats

1 cup raisins

1. Position an oven rack so that the cookies will bake in the middle of the oven and pre-heat the oven to 350 degrees F. Line a baking sheet with kitchen parchment or a silicone baking mat and set aside.

2. In a bowl, combine the flour, baking soda, and salt. Whisk to mix well and set aside.

3. In another bowl, combine the butter and sugars and beat with an electric mixer at medium speed until the mixture is light and

fluffy, about 5 minutes. Add the egg and vanilla and blend well. Add the flour mixture and mix at low speed just until incorporated. Stir in the oats, about 1 cup at a time, just until incorporated, then stir in the raisins.

4. Using a #20 (¹/4-cup) ice-cream scoop, scoop up level portions of dough and place them about 3 inches apart on the lined baking sheet until the sheet is full. (Cover the remaining dough tightly with plastic wrap to prevent drying out and set aside until forming the next batch of cookies.)

5. Transfer the baking sheet to the oven and bake until the edges of the cookies are lightly browned and the centers are set, about 18 minutes.

6. Remove the baking sheet to a wire rack to cool for a few minutes, then using a spatula, transfer the cookies directly to the rack to cool completely.

7. Repeat the forming and baking process until the dough is used up.

The cookies may be stored in an airtight container at room temperature for up to 3 days.

VARIATIONS

Oatmeal Scotchies *Substitute butterscotch chips for the raisins.*

Oatmeal Chippers *Substitute chopped semisweet chocolate or semisweet chocolate chips for the raisins.*

Oatmeal Nutties *Substitute peanut butter chips for the raisins.*

Oatmeal Bitties *Substitute English toffee bits for the raisins.*

We prefer these smooth and chewy cookies made with creamy peanut butter. If you'd like some crunch, use chunky peanut butter and/or stir about 1/2 cup coarsely chopped dry-roasted peanuts into the dough after adding the flour mixture. Chocolate and peanut butter make a fabulous team, so try the chocolate-dipped variation.

peanut butter
cookies / *Makes about 1 dozen large cookies*

1¹/2 cups all-purpose flour
1/2 teaspoon baking soda
1/2 teaspoon salt
1 cup creamy peanut butter, at room temperature
1/2 cup (1 stick) unsalted butter, at room temperature
3/4 cup granulated sugar
3/4 cup firmly packed light brown sugar
1 large egg, at room temperature

1. Position an oven rack so that the cookies will bake in the middle of the oven and preheat the oven to 350 degrees F. Line a baking sheet with kitchen parchment or a silicone baking mat and set aside.

2. In a bowl, combine the flour, baking soda, and salt. Whisk to mix well and set aside.

3. In another bowl, combine the peanut butter, butter, and sugars and beat with an electric mixer at medium speed until the mixture is smooth and creamy, about 5 minutes. Add the egg and blend well. Add the flour mixture and mix at low speed just until incorporated.

4. Using a #20 (1/4-cup) ice-cream scoop, scoop up a level portion of dough. Roll the dough portion between your palms to form a ball, then place the dough ball on the lined

baking sheet. Repeat with the remaining dough, placing the balls about 3 inches apart, until the sheet is full. (Cover the remaining dough tightly with plastic wrap to prevent drying out and set aside until forming the next batch of cookies.) Press down on the dough balls with your fingertips to form each ball into a round about $1/2$ inch thick and smooth the edges of each round. If desired, use a fork to press the traditional crisscross marks in the middle of each round.

5. Transfer the baking sheet to the oven and bake until the cookies are lightly browned, about 12 minutes.

6. Remove the baking sheet to a wire rack to cool for a few minutes, then using a spatula, transfer the cookies directly to the rack to cool completely.

7. Repeat the forming and baking process until the dough is used up.

The cookies may be stored in an airtight container at room temperature for up to 3 days.

VARIATION
Chocolate-Dipped Peanut Butter Cookies *See page 21.*

Early New England cookbooks dubbed these perennial favorites schneckennoodles, leading some food historians to speculate a corruption of the German word *Schneckennudeln,* or "crinkly noodles." Whatever the origin, and in any language, these simple sugar cookies with cinnamon-dusted crinkled tops are sure-fire winners with coffee or tea.

snickerdoodles / *Makes about 1 dozen large cookies*

2 1/2 cups all-purpose flour

2 teaspoons cream of tartar

1 teaspoon baking soda

1/2 teaspoon salt

1 cup (2 sticks) unsalted butter, at room temperature

1 1/2 cups plus 2 tablespoons granulated sugar

2 large eggs, at room temperature

2 teaspoons pure vanilla extract

1 teaspoon ground cinnamon

1. Position an oven rack so that the cookies will bake in the middle of the oven and pre-heat the oven to 350 degrees F. Line a baking sheet with kitchen parchment or a silicone baking mat and set aside.

2. In a bowl, combine the flour, cream of tartar, baking soda, and salt. Whisk to mix well and set aside.

3. In another bowl, combine the butter and 1 1/2 cups of the sugar and beat with an electric mixer at medium speed until the mixture is light and fluffy, about 5 minutes. Add the eggs and vanilla and blend well. Add the flour mixture, about 1 cup at a time, and mix at low speed just until incorporated.

4. In a shallow bowl, combine the remaining 2 tablespoons sugar and the cinnamon and mix well.

5. Using a #20 (1/4-cup) ice-cream scoop, scoop up a level portion of dough. Roll the dough portion between your palms to form a ball. Roll the dough ball in the sugar-cinnamon mixture to coat evenly. Place the dough ball on the lined baking sheet. Repeat with the remaining dough, placing the balls about 3 inches apart, until the sheet is full. (Cover the remaining dough tightly with plastic wrap to prevent drying out and set aside until forming the next batch of cookies.)

6. Transfer the baking sheet to the oven and bake until the cookies form fine cracks and are lightly browned around the edges, about 17 minutes.

7. Remove the baking sheet to a wire rack to cool for a few minutes, then using a spatula, transfer the cookies directly to the rack to cool completely.

8. Repeat the forming and baking process until the dough is used up.

The cookies may be stored in an airtight container at room temperature for up to 3 days.

A takeoff on Linzertorte, which originated in Linz, Austria, these delicately spiced almond cookies sandwiched with raspberry jam are lighter and crispier than their famous ancestor, but equally delicious. The cookies get soggy very quickly from the jam, so serve them shortly after assembling.

linzer
cookies / *Makes about 1 dozen large cookies*

2 cups all-purpose flour

1/2 teaspoon baking powder

1/2 teaspoon salt

1/2 teaspoon ground cinnamon

1/4 teaspoon ground cloves

1 cup almonds, lightly toasted (see page 16)

1 cup granulated sugar

1 cup (2 sticks) unsalted butter, at room temperature

1 tablespoon finely grated or minced fresh lemon zest

1 large egg, at room temperature

1/2 teaspoon pure almond extract

Powdered sugar for dusting

About 3/4 cup seedless raspberry jam

1. In a bowl, combine the flour, baking powder, salt, cinnamon, and cloves. Whisk to mix well and set aside.

2. In a food processor, combine the toasted almonds and 1/4 cup of the granulated sugar and process until the nuts are very finely ground. Set aside.

3. In another bowl, combine the butter, the remaining 3/4 cup granulated sugar, and the lemon zest and beat with an electric mixer at

medium speed until the mixture is light and fluffy, about 5 minutes. Add the egg and almond extract and blend well. Add the ground almonds and mix well. Add the flour mixture, about 1 cup at a time, and mix at low speed just until incorporated.

4. Divide the dough into 4 equal pieces. Working with one piece at a time, form it into a flat disk about 1 inch thick, then roll it out between 2 pieces of waxed paper or plastic wrap to a thickness of slightly more than 1/8 inch. Repeat with the remaining pieces of dough. Stack the pieces of rolled dough (leave them in the waxed paper or plastic wrap) and refrigerate until well chilled and very firm, at least 2 hours.

5. Position an oven rack so that the cookies will bake in the middle of the oven and pre-heat the oven to 350 degrees F. Line a baking sheet with kitchen parchment or a silicone baking mat and set aside.

6. Working with one piece at a time, remove a piece of rolled dough from the refrigerator (keep the remaining pieces refrigerated until using). Peel off the top sheet of waxed paper or plastic wrap. Working as quickly as possible while the dough is firm, and using a 4-inch round or fluted round cookie cutter, cut out as many rounds as possible from the dough. Then using a 2-inch round cutter, cut out and remove a circle from the center of half of the rounds. Peel the cutout rounds, both the solid ones and the ones with the centers removed, from the waxed paper or plastic wrap and place them about 1 inch apart on the lined baking sheet until the sheet is full. (Wrap and save the remaining dough scraps, including the removed centers, for later use.)

7. Transfer the baking sheet to the oven and bake until the cookies are lightly browned around the edges, about 15 minutes.

8. Remove the baking sheet to a wire rack to cool for a few minutes, then using a spatula, transfer the cookies directly to the rack to cool completely.

9. Repeat the cutting and baking process with the remaining pieces of rolled dough. Then gather all the dough scraps and, in the same manner, form into disks, roll out, place in a freezer to chill quickly until firm, and cut out and bake as many cookies as possible, repeat-ing the process until the dough is used up.

At this point, the cookies may be stored in an airtight container at room temperature for up to 3 days.

10. Shortly before serving, assemble the cook-ies. Sift a light dusting of powdered sugar over the cookies with the centers cut out. Turn the solid cookies top-side down and evenly spread each cookie with about 1 table-spoon of raspberry jam. Place a sugar-dusted cookie on top of each jam-spread cookie and press together gently to make a sandwich.

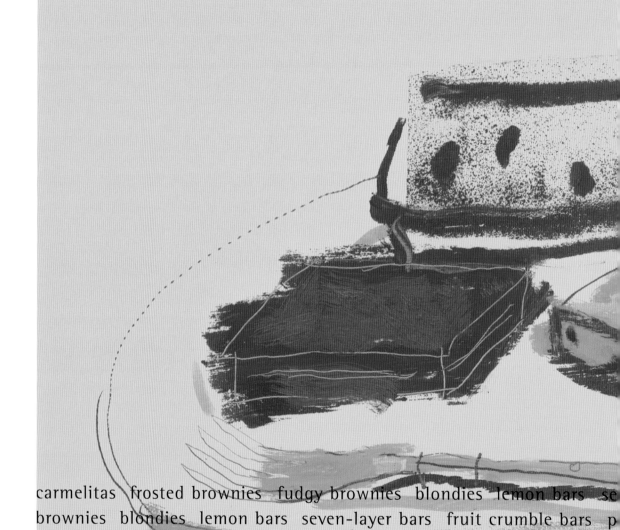

carmelitas frosted brownies fudgy brownies blondies lemon bars se
brownies blondies lemon bars seven-layer bars fruit crumble bars p
layer bars fruit crumble bars pecan bars carmelitas frosted brownies
bars carmelitas frosted brownies fudgy brownies blondies lemon ba

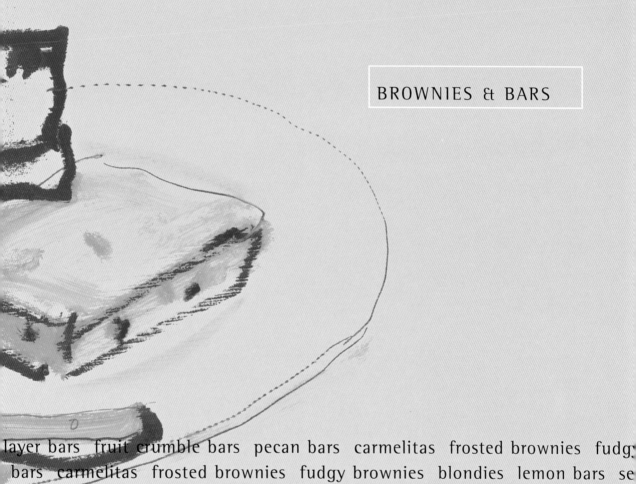

layer bars fruit crumble bars pecan bars carmelitas frosted brownies fudg
bars carmelitas frosted brownies fudgy brownies blondies lemon bars se
gy brownies blondies lemon bars seven-layer bars fruit crumble bars peca
even-layer bars fruit crumble bars pecan bars carmelitas frosted brownies

These chewy caramel-nut-chocolate delights, which we rediscovered in several upscale coffeehouses, are based on an entry from a Pillsbury Bake-Off® in the 1960s. When we don't have time to make our own caramel sauce, we like to use Mrs. Richardson's Butterscotch Caramel Topping.

carmelitas / *Makes 1 dozen large bars*

Solid vegetable shortening, at room temperature, for greasing

2 cups quick-cooking rolled oats

2 cups all-purpose flour

1½ cups firmly packed light brown sugar

1 teaspoon baking soda

½ teaspoon salt

1 cup (2 sticks) unsalted butter, melted

10 ounces semisweet or bittersweet chocolate, coarsely chopped, or 1½ cups semisweet chocolate chips

1 cup pecans or walnuts, lightly toasted (see page 16) and coarsely chopped

1 cup caramel sauce (a favorite recipe made with cream) or commercial caramel topping

1. Position an oven rack so that the carmelitas will bake in the middle of the oven and preheat the oven to 350 degrees F. Using a pastry brush, grease the bottom and sides of a 13-by-9-inch baking pan with shortening. Set aside.

2. In a bowl, combine the oats, flour, brown sugar, baking soda, and salt. Stir to mix well. Add the butter and mix until well blended. Distribute half of the mixture in the prepared pan and press gently with your fingertips to form an even layer. Reserve the remaining mixture for later use. →

3. Transfer the pan to the oven and bake for 10 minutes.

4. Remove the pan from the oven. Sprinkle the chopped chocolate or chocolate chips and the toasted nuts evenly over the crust, then drizzle evenly with the caramel sauce. Distribute the reserved oat mixture over the top and press gently with your fingertips to form an even layer.

5. Return the pan to the oven and continue baking until the topping is golden brown, about 25 minutes longer.

6. Remove the pan to a wire rack to cool completely, then cut into 12 equal bars.

The carmelitas may be covered tightly and stored at room temperature for up to 2 days.

For traditional brownie lovers, here's our rendition of moist, chewy treats topped with a thick layer of smooth, fudgy frosting. We like to use a high-quality chocolate, such as Callebaut, Scharffen Berger, or Valrhona, for both the brownies and frosting. The brownies are also delicious served unfrosted.

frosted
brownies / *Makes 1 dozen large brownies*

Solid vegetable shortening, at room temperature, for greasing

brownies

8 ounces unsweetened chocolate, coarsely chopped

1/2 cup (1 stick) unsalted butter, cut into small pieces

3 cups granulated sugar

4 large eggs, at room temperature

2 teaspoons pure vanilla extract

1/2 teaspoon salt

2 cups bleached all-purpose flour

2 cups pecans or walnuts, lightly toasted (see page 16) and coarsely chopped (optional)

fudgy chocolate frosting

4 ounces unsweetened chocolate, coarsely chopped

6 tablespoons (3/4 stick) unsalted butter, cut into small pieces

3 cups powdered sugar

2 tablespoons milk, or more if needed

1 teaspoon pure vanilla extract

1/8 teaspoon salt →

frosted brownies

1. Position an oven rack so that the brownies will bake in the middle of the oven and preheat the oven to 350 degrees F. Using a pastry brush, grease the bottom and sides of a 13-by-9-inch baking pan with shortening. Set aside.

2. To make the brownies, in a large stainless-steel bowl, combine the chopped chocolate with the butter. Set the bowl in a large skillet or shallow saucepan containing about 1 inch of barely simmering water and stir the chocolate mixture gently until melted and smooth. Remove the bowl from the heat and set aside to cool for about 10 minutes.

3. Add the granulated sugar, eggs, vanilla, and salt to the cooled chocolate mixture and mix until well blended. Add the flour and mix gently just until incorporated. Stir in the toasted nuts (if using). Scrape the batter into the prepared pan and spread evenly.

4. Transfer the pan to the oven and bake until a wooden skewer inserted halfway between the edge of the pan and the center of the brownies comes out only slightly moist with a few crumbs attached, about 30 minutes.

5. Remove the pan to a wire rack to cool completely before frosting the brownies.

6. To make the frosting, in a large stainless-steel bowl, combine the chopped chocolate with the butter. Set the bowl in a large skillet or shallow saucepan containing about 1 inch of barely simmering water and stir the chocolate mixture gently until melted and smooth. Remove the bowl from the heat and set aside to cool for about 10 minutes.

7. Add 1 cup of the powdered sugar, 2 tablespoons milk, the vanilla, and the salt to the cooled chocolate mixture and beat with a hand mixer at medium speed until smooth. Add the remaining 2 cups powdered sugar, about 1 cup at a time, and continue beating at medium speed until the frosting is smooth and spreadable. Add a little more milk, about 1 teaspoon at a time, if necessary to achieve a spreadable consistency, but do not let the frosting get too thin.

8. Spread the frosting over the cooled brownies, smoothing the top with a flexible frosting spatula. Cut into 12 equal bars. (When slicing, you will need to wipe the knife blade clean after each cut.)

The brownies may be covered tightly and stored at room temperature for up to 2 days.

If you enjoy dense and gooey brownies, here's our favorite version. For ultimate flavor, use only the best-quality chocolate. Since these brownies are somewhat difficult to cut and serve from the pan, you may wish to line the pan with aluminum foil as described on page 18. And if you can resist eating them at once, they taste even better the day after baking.

fudgy brownies / *Makes 1 dozen large brownies*

Solid vegetable shortening, at room temperature, for greasing

8 ounces semisweet chocolate, coarsely chopped

4 ounces unsweetened chocolate, coarsely chopped

1 1/4 cups (2 1/2 sticks) unsalted butter, cut into small pieces

2 1/4 cups granulated sugar

1/2 teaspoon salt

2 teaspoons pure vanilla extract

5 large eggs, at room temperature

3/4 cup bleached all-purpose flour

2 cups pecans or other nuts, lightly toasted (see page 16) and coarsely chopped (optional)

1. Position an oven rack so that the brownies will bake in the middle of the oven and preheat the oven to 350 degrees F. Using a pastry brush, grease the bottom and sides of a 13-by-9-inch baking pan with shortening. Set aside.

2. In a large stainless-steel bowl, combine the chopped chocolates with the butter. Set the bowl in a large skillet or shallow saucepan containing about 1 inch of barely simmering water and stir the chocolate mixture gently until melted and smooth.

the edge of the pan and the center of the brownies comes out only slightly moist with a few crumbs attached, about 40 minutes.

4. Remove the pan to a wire rack to cool completely, then cut into 12 equal bars. (When slicing, you will need to wipe the knife blade clean after each cut.)

The brownies may be covered tightly and stored at room temperature for up to 2 days.

VARIATIONS

Espresso Brownies *Add 3 table-spoons instant espresso powder, preferably Medaglia d'Oro brand (available in Italian grocery stores and upscale supermarkets), to the melted chocolate-butter mixture after removing from the heat and stir until dissolved.*

Raspberry Brownies *Stir 1/2 cup seedless raspberry jam into the melted chocolate-butter mixture after removing from the heat.*

Remove the bowl from the heat, add the sugar, salt, and vanilla, and stir until well blended. Add the eggs, one at a time, and stir until each is well incorporated before adding the next. Add the flour and beat with a spoon until the mixture is smooth and glossy, about 1 minute. Stir in the toasted nuts (if using). Scrape the batter into the prepared pan and spread evenly.

3. Transfer the pan to the oven and bake until the edges of the brownies just begin to pull away from the sides of the pan and a wooden skewer inserted halfway between

Also known as butterscotch brownies and blonde brownies, these butterscotch-flavored bars are quick and easy to make— a spontaneous delight! When served warm, topped with a scoop of vanilla ice cream and a drizzle of butterscotch sauce, they become an indulgent dessert. Chocoholics will delight in our "freckled" variation.

blondies / Makes 1 dozen large blondies

Solid vegetable shortening, at room temperature, for greasing

2 cups all-purpose flour

1 teaspoon baking powder

1/2 teaspoon salt

3/4 cup (11/2 sticks) unsalted butter, melted and cooled slightly

2 cups firmly packed light brown sugar

2 large eggs, at room temperature

2 teaspoons pure vanilla extract

1 cup pecans, lightly toasted (see page 16) and coarsely chopped

1 cup butterscotch chips

1. Position an oven rack so that the blondies will bake in the middle of the oven and preheat the oven to 350 degrees F. Using a pastry brush, grease the bottom and sides of a 13-by-9-inch baking pan with shortening. Set aside.

2. In a bowl, combine the flour, baking powder, and salt. Whisk to mix well and set aside.

3. In another bowl, combine the butter, brown sugar, eggs, and vanilla and mix until well blended. Add the flour mixture and mix gently just until incorporated. Stir in the toasted pecans and the butterscotch chips. Scrape the batter into the prepared pan and spread evenly.

4. Transfer the pan to the oven and bake until a wooden skewer inserted into the center of the blondies comes out clean, about 30 minutes.

5. Remove the pan to a wire rack to cool completely, then cut into 12 equal bars.

The blondies may be covered tightly and stored at room temperature for up to 2 days.

VARIATION

Freckled Blondies *Substitute semi-sweet chocolate chips for the butter-scotch chips.*

These bars, with their shortbread base and a tangy topping that recalls lemon curd, are a perennial favorite. If using Meyer lemons, reduce the sugar in the topping to $2^{1/2}$ cups.

lemon
bars / *Makes 1 dozen large bars*

Solid vegetable shortening, at room temperature, for greasing

crust
1 cup (2 sticks) unsalted butter, at room temperature
$1/2$ cup granulated sugar
$1/4$ teaspoon salt
2 cups bleached all-purpose flour

topping
6 large eggs
3 cups granulated sugar
$1/2$ cup all-purpose flour
Pinch of salt
1 cup freshly squeezed lemon juice
2 teaspoons finely grated or minced fresh lemon zest

Powdered sugar for dusting

1. Position an oven rack so that the bars will bake in the middle of the oven and preheat the oven to 350 degrees F. Using a pastry brush, grease the bottom and sides of a 13-by-9-inch baking pan with shortening. Set aside.

2. To make the crust, in a bowl, beat the butter with an electric mixer at medium speed until soft and creamy, about 45 seconds. Add the sugar and salt and mix until well blended. Add the flour, about 1 cup at a time, and mix until the dough is smooth, about 2 minutes. Scrape the dough into the prepared pan and spread evenly. Place a piece of plastic wrap over the dough and press on the dough $\rightarrow$

5. When the crust is done, remove the pan from the oven and reduce the oven temperature to 325 degrees F. Pour the topping mixture evenly onto the crust. Return the pan to the oven and bake until the topping feels set when lightly touched in the center with your fingertip and no longer wobbles in the center when the pan is shaken, about 30 minutes.

6. Remove the pan to a wire rack to cool completely, then cut into 12 equal bars.

7. The bars may be covered tightly and stored at room temperature for up to several hours, or refrigerated for up to 2 days. Just before serving, sift a light dusting of powdered sugar over them.

through the plastic wrap with your fingertips to form a smooth, even layer on the bottom of the pan. Remove the plastic wrap.

3. Transfer the pan to the oven and bake until the crust is golden brown, about 20 minutes.

4. Meanwhile, to make the topping, in a bowl, combine the eggs, sugar, flour, and salt and whisk or beat with a hand mixer until well blended. Add the lemon juice and zest and blend until smooth.

For these supersweet and gooey nostalgic treats, we combine the butter and crumb "layers" which makes for a better crust. When made without butterscotch chips, the bars are called *Hello Dollies*. We've dubbed our Hawaiian variation *Hula Dollies*, with island flavors of coffee and macadamia nuts.

seven-layer
bars / *Makes 1 dozen large bars*

1/2 cup (1 stick) unsalted butter, melted

2 cups graham-cracker crumbs, preferably cinnamon flavored
  (pulverized in a food processor from about 15 double crackers)

1 1/2 cups sweetened shredded coconut

1 1/2 cups pecans, lightly toasted (see page 16) and coarsely chopped

1 1/2 cups semisweet chocolate chips

1 1/2 cups butterscotch chips

1 1/2 cans (14 ounces each) sweetened condensed milk (2 2/3 cups)

1. Position an oven rack so that the bars will bake in the middle of the oven and preheat the oven to 350 degrees F.

2. In a bowl, combine the butter and graham-cracker crumbs and stir until well blended. Distribute the mixture evenly in a 13-by-9-inch baking pan and press with your fingertips to form a smooth, compact layer. Sprinkle the coconut evenly over the crumb layer, then repeat with the toasted pecans, the chocolate chips, and finally the butterscotch chips. Pour the condensed milk evenly over the top.

3. Transfer the pan to the oven and bake until the milk in the center of the pan is bubbling and golden, about 35 minutes.

4. Remove the pan to a wire rack to cool completely, then cut into 12 equal bars.

The bars may be covered tightly and stored at room temperature for up to 2 days. →

VARIATIONS

Hello Dollies *Omit the butterscotch chips.*

Hula Dollies *Use plain graham crackers. Substitute macadamia nuts for the pecans. Substitute coarsely chopped white chocolate or white chocolate chips for the semisweet chocolate chips and omit the butterscotch chips. Dissolve 2 tablespoons instant espresso powder, preferably Medaglia d'Oro brand (available in Italian grocery stores and upscale supermarkets), in 1 tablespoon hot water, then stir thoroughly into the condensed milk before pouring it over the top.*

In coffeehouses, these bars, reminiscent of a crumbly fruit crisp, are usually offered with a filling of apricots, blueberries, or cranberries. Other dried fruits, such as apples, dates, figs, prunes, raisins, or sour cherries, would make a nice filling, too. Tart fruits will need the full amount of granulated sugar. For sweeter fruits, start with the minimum, then taste and add more sugar if needed before pureeing.

fruit crumble
bars / *Makes 1 dozen large bars*

4 cups dried fruit (see recipe introduction)

1/2 to 1 cup granulated sugar, depending upon sweetness of fruit
 (see recipe introduction)

Solid vegetable shortening, at room temperature, for greasing

3 cups old-fashioned (not quick-cooking) rolled oats

11/2 cups all-purpose flour

1 cup firmly packed light brown sugar

11/2 teaspoons ground cinnamon

3/4 teaspoon salt

3/4 teaspoon baking soda

1 cup (2 sticks) unsalted butter, melted

1. In a saucepan, combine the dried fruit, granulated sugar, and 2 cups water. Place over medium heat and cook, stirring frequently, until the fruit is plumped and tender and the liquid is absorbed; the cooking time will vary with the type and dryness of the fruit. Remove from the heat and let cool for a few minutes, then transfer the fruit to a food

processor and pulse a few times to puree coarsely. Set aside.

2. Position an oven rack so that the bars will bake in the middle of the oven and pre-heat the oven to 350 degrees F. Using a pastry brush, grease the bottom and sides of a 13-by-9-inch baking pan with shortening. Set aside.

3. In a bowl, combine the oats, flour, brown sugar, cinnamon, salt, and baking soda. Stir to mix well. Add the butter and mix until well blended and crumbly. Remove 2 cups of the oat mixture and set aside. Distribute the remaining oat mixture in the prepared pan and press gently to form an even layer. Spoon the pureed fruit over the layer and spread evenly. Distribute the reserved 2 cups oat mixture evenly over the fruit and press gently to form a top crust.

4. Transfer the pan to the oven and bake until the surface of the bars is lightly browned and set, about 30 minutes.

5. Remove the pan to a wire rack to cool completely, then cut into 12 equal bars.

The bars may be covered tightly and stored at room temperature for up to 2 days.

Easier than pie and chock-full of pecan flavor, there's just nuttin' better than these! If you wish to dress them up a bit, after they have cooled completely, drizzle melted bitter-sweet chocolate (see page 21) over the bars to create a zigzag pattern.

pecan
bars / *Makes 1 dozen large bars*

Solid vegetable shortening, at room temperature, for greasing

crust
1 cup (2 sticks) unsalted butter, at room temperature
1/2 cup granulated sugar
1/4 teaspoon salt
2 cups bleached all-purpose flour

topping
11/2 cups firmly packed light brown sugar
1/2 cup light corn syrup
1/2 cup (1 stick) unsalted butter
1/4 cup heavy (whipping) cream
2 teaspoons pure vanilla extract
4 cups pecans, lightly toasted (see page 16) and coarsely chopped

1. Position an oven rack so that the bars will bake in the middle of the oven and pre-heat the oven to 350 degrees F. Using a pastry brush, grease the bottom and sides of a 13-by-9-inch baking pan with shortening. Set aside.

2. To make the crust, in a bowl, beat the butter with an electric mixer at medium speed until soft and creamy, about 45 seconds. Add the sugar and salt and mix until well blended. Add the flour, about 1 cup at a time, and mix until the dough is smooth, about 2 minutes.

Scrape the dough into the prepared pan and spread evenly. Place a piece of plastic wrap over the dough and press on the dough through the plastic wrap with your fingertips to form a smooth, even layer on the bottom of the pan. Remove the plastic wrap.

3. Transfer the pan to the oven and bake until the crust is golden brown, about 20 minutes.

4. Remove the pan to a wire rack and set aside.

5. To make the topping, in a saucepan, combine the brown sugar, corn syrup, and butter. Place over medium heat and bring the mixture to a full boil, stirring constantly. Remove from the heat, add the cream and vanilla, and mix until well blended. Add the toasted pecans and mix well.

6. Pour the topping mixture onto the crust and spread evenly. Return the pan to the oven and bake until the topping is bubbling all over, about 25 minutes.

7. Remove the pan to a wire rack to cool completely.

8. Cut into 12 equal bars. Trim off the hard outer edges, if desired.

The bars may be covered tightly and stored at room temperature for up to 2 days.

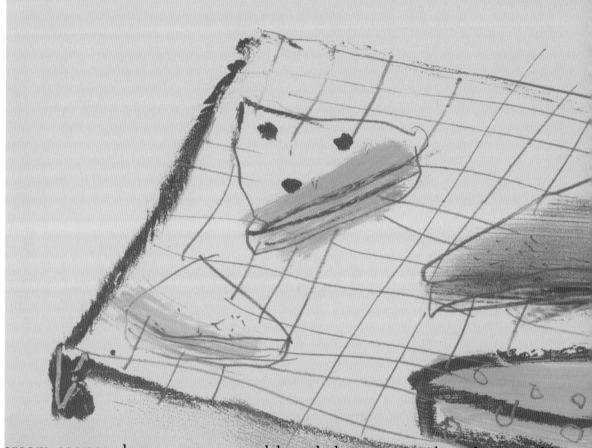

cream scones lemon-poppy seed bread banana nut bread pumpkin sp
nut bread pumpkin spice bread crumb-topped coffee cake cream scor
coffee cake cream scones lemon-poppy seed bread banana nut bread
bread banana nut bread pumpkin spice bread crumb-topped coffee ca

SCONES, QUICK BREADS & COFFEE CAKE

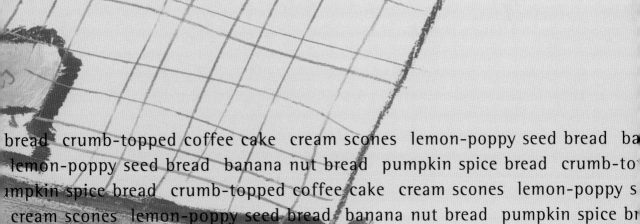

bread   crumb-topped coffee cake   cream scones   lemon-poppy seed bread   ba
lemon-poppy seed bread   banana nut bread   pumpkin spice bread   crumb-to
umpkin spice bread   crumb-topped coffee cake   cream scones   lemon-poppy s
cream scones   lemon-poppy seed bread   banana nut bread   pumpkin spice br

For old-fashioned goodness in every bite, be sure to mix and knead the dough quickly and gently, and avoid overbaking. We enjoy these rich, crumbly biscuits with citrus curd or fruit jam and cups of strong Earl Grey tea.

cream
scones / *Makes 8 large scones*

3 cups all-purpose flour

6 tablespoons granulated sugar

4 teaspoons baking powder

3/4 teaspoon salt

3/4 cup (1 1/2 sticks) cold unsalted butter, cut into small pieces

1 cup heavy cream

3/4 cup dried currants, coarsely chopped sweetened dried cranberries, or diced crystallized ginger

1. Position an oven rack so that the scones will bake in the middle of the oven and preheat the oven to 400 degrees F. Line a baking sheet with kitchen parchment or a silicone baking mat and set aside.

2. In a bowl or food processor, combine the flour, sugar, baking powder, and salt and whisk or pulse to blend well. Add the cold butter and mix with your fingertips or pulse in the food processor just until the mixture resembles coarse bread crumbs. If using a food processor, transfer the mixture to a bowl.

Add the cream and the currants, cranberries, or ginger. Stir just until the mixture sticks together (it will be crumbly).

3. Transfer the mixture to a lightly floured work surface and knead gently and quickly just until it comes together, about 30 seconds. Shape the dough into an even, flat round that is 1 inch thick and about 8 inches in diameter. Using a floured knife, cut the dough into 8 equal wedges. Place the wedges about 2 inches apart on the lined baking sheet. →

4. Bake until the scones are lightly golden and offer only slight resistance when lightly touched in their centers with your fingertip, 18 to 20 minutes.

5. Remove the baking sheet to a work surface, then using a spatula, transfer the scones to a wire rack to cool for a few minutes. Serve warm or at room temperature.

The scones may be stored in an airtight container at room temperature for up to 3 days.

We enjoy this tangy loaf, glazed with lemon syrup, with a perfect pot of afternoon tea. Wrapped in clear cellophane and tied with a yellow satin or plaid ribbon, the homey bread makes a great gift.

lemon–poppy seed
bread / *Makes 12 large slices*

1 cup buttermilk or plain yogurt (not fat free)

1/4 cup poppy seeds

Solid vegetable shortening, at room temperature, for greasing

2 1/2 cups all-purpose flour

2 1/2 teaspoons baking powder

1/2 teaspoon salt

1/2 cup (1 stick) unsalted butter, melted and cooled slightly

1 1/2 cups granulated sugar

2 large eggs, at room temperature

2 tablespoons finely grated or minced fresh lemon zest

1 tablespoon pure lemon extract

lemon glaze

6 tablespoons granulated sugar

1/4 cup freshly squeezed lemon juice

1. In a bowl or glass measuring cup, combine the buttermilk or yogurt and poppy seeds and let stand for about 1 hour to soften the seeds.

2. Position an oven rack so that the bread will bake in the middle of the oven and preheat the oven to 350 degrees F. Using a pastry brush, grease the bottom and sides of a 9-by-5-inch loaf pan with shortening. Line the bottom of the pan with kitchen parchment. Set aside.

3. In a bowl, combine the flour, baking powder, and salt. Whisk to mix well and set aside. →

4. In another bowl, combine the butter, sugar, eggs, lemon zest, lemon extract, and buttermilk–poppy seed mixture and mix until well blended. Add the flour mixture, about 1 cup at a time, and mix gently just until incorporated. Scrape the batter into the prepared pan.

5. Transfer the pan to the oven and bake until a wooden skewer inserted into the center of the bread comes out clean, about 1 hour.

6. Meanwhile, to make the glaze, in a small saucepan, combine the sugar and lemon juice. Place over medium heat and stir until the sugar is dissolved. Remove from the heat and set aside.

7. When the bread is done, remove the pan to a wire rack. Pierce the top of the bread all over with a wooden skewer. Using a pastry brush, brush the glaze all over the top of the bread until absorbed. Set aside to cool completely.

8. When the bread has cooled, run the blade of a thin, flexible metal spatula or knife all around the sides of the bread to loosen it from the pan. Place one of your hands on top of the bread, invert the pan with both hands, lift off the pan, and peel off the parchment.

9. Wrap the bread tightly in plastic wrap and store at room temperature overnight (for better flavor and easier slicing) or for up to 1 week. Slice into 12 equal slices just before serving.

85

Almost everyone likes banana bread, and our version, studded with macadamia nuts and topped with a sweet-hot crunch, may become a new favorite, especially when it is served alongside a cup of Kona coffee. For maximum flavor and sweetness, make sure the bananas are overripe—the skins should be covered with spots or even completely black.

banana
nut bread / *Makes 12 large slices*

Solid vegetable shortening, at room temperature, for greasing

2 1/2 cups all-purpose flour

2 1/2 teaspoons baking powder

1/2 teaspoon salt

1/2 cup (1 stick) unsalted butter, melted and cooled slightly

2 cups firmly packed light brown sugar

2 large eggs, at room temperature

2 cups mashed overripe bananas (see recipe introduction)

2 teaspoons pure vanilla extract

1 cup macadamia nuts, lightly toasted (see page 16) and coarsely chopped

ginger crunch

1/4 cup granulated sugar

1 tablespoon finely minced fresh ginger

1. Position an oven rack so that the bread will bake in the middle of the oven and preheat the oven to 350 degrees F. Using a pastry brush, grease the bottom and sides of a 9-by-5-inch loaf pan with shortening. Line the bottom of the pan with kitchen parchment. Set aside.

2. In a bowl, combine the flour, baking powder, and salt. Whisk to mix well and set aside.

3. In another bowl, combine the butter, brown sugar, eggs, mashed bananas, and vanilla and mix until well blended. Add the flour mixture, about 1 cup at a time, and mix gently just until incorporated. Stir in the toasted nuts. Scrape the batter into the prepared pan.

4. Transfer the pan to the oven and bake just until the top of the bread is set, about 30 minutes.

5. Meanwhile, to make the ginger crunch, in a small bowl, combine the granulated sugar and ginger and mix well.

6. Remove the pan from the oven and sprinkle the ginger crunch mixture evenly over the top of the bread. Return the pan to the oven and continue baking until a wooden skewer inserted into the center of the bread comes out barely clean, about 1 hour longer.

7. Remove the pan to a wire rack and set aside to cool completely.

8. When the bread has cooled, run the blade of a thin, flexible metal spatula or knife all around the sides of the bread to loosen it from the pan. Place one of your hands on top of the bread, invert the pan with both hands, lift off the pan, and peel off the parchment.

9. Wrap the bread tightly in plastic wrap and store at room temperature overnight (for better flavor and easier slicing) or for up to 1 week. Slice into 12 equal slices just before serving.

This spicy bread, moist with pumpkin and plump raisins, captures the color and flavor of autumn in every bite. Spread slices with softened cream cheese for a satisfying accompaniment to coffee or tea.

pumpkin spice
bread / *Makes 12 large slices*

Solid vegetable shortening, at room temperature, for greasing

2 1/2 cups all-purpose flour

2 1/2 teaspoons baking powder

1/2 teaspoon salt

1 tablespoon ground cinnamon

1 teaspoon ground cloves

1/2 teaspoon freshly grated nutmeg

1/2 cup (1 stick) unsalted butter, melted and cooled slightly

2 cups firmly packed light brown sugar

2 large eggs, at room temperature

1 1/2 cups canned pumpkin puree

1 cup raisins

1. Position an oven rack so that the bread will bake in the middle of the oven and preheat the oven to 350 degrees F. Using a pastry brush, grease the bottom and sides of a 9-by-5-inch loaf pan with shortening. Line the bottom of the pan with kitchen parchment. Set aside.

2. In a bowl, combine the flour, baking powder, salt, cinnamon, cloves, and nutmeg. Whisk to mix well and set aside.

3. In another bowl, combine the butter, brown sugar, eggs, and pumpkin puree and mix until well blended. Add the flour mixture, about 1 cup at a time, and mix gently just until incorporated. Stir in the raisins. Scrape the batter into the prepared pan.

4. Transfer the pan to the oven and bake until a wooden skewer inserted into the center of the bread comes out clean, about 1 hour and 15 minutes.

5. Remove the pan to a wire rack and set aside to cool completely.

6. When the bread has cooled, run the blade of a thin, flexible metal spatula or knife all around the sides of the bread to loosen it from the pan. Place one of your hands on top of the bread, invert the pan with both hands, lift off the pan, and peel off the parchment.

Wrap the bread tightly in plastic wrap and store at room temperature overnight (for better flavor and easier slicing) or for up to 1 week. Slice into 12 equal slices just before serving.

These days, almost every coffeehouse offers a version of old-fashioned crumb cake. Here's ours, made tangy with buttermilk or yogurt. We prefer the homey cake still warm from the oven with steaming mugs of robust coffee.

crumb-topped
coffee cake / *Makes 12 large pieces*

Solid vegetable shortening, at room temperature, for greasing

crumb topping

2 cups bleached all-purpose flour

1 cup firmly packed light brown sugar

1 tablespoon ground cinnamon

1/4 teaspoon salt

3/4 cup (1 1/2 sticks) unsalted butter, melted and cooled slightly

coffee cake

4 cups bleached all-purpose flour

1 cup firmly packed light brown sugar

1 cup granulated sugar

4 teaspoons baking powder

1 teaspoon salt

1/2 cup (1 stick) unsalted butter, melted and cooled slightly

4 large eggs, at room temperature

1 tablespoon pure vanilla extract

2 cups buttermilk or plain yogurt (not fat free), at room temperature

Powdered sugar for dusting (optional) →

1. Position an oven rack so that the cake will bake in the middle of the oven and pre-heat the oven to 350 degrees F. Using a pastry brush, generously grease a 13-by-9-inch baking pan with shortening and set aside.

2. To make the topping, in a bowl, combine the flour, brown sugar, cinnamon, and salt and stir to mix well. Stir in the melted butter, then rub the mixture between your fingertips to form large, coarse crumbs. Set aside.

3. To make the cake, in a bowl, combine the flour, sugars, baking powder, and salt and whisk to mix well. Add the butter, eggs, vanilla, and buttermilk or yogurt and beat with an electric mixer at medium speed until smooth and creamy, about 2 minutes.

4. Scrape the batter into the prepared pan and smooth the surface with a rubber spatula. Distribute the reserved topping mixture evenly over the top.

5. Transfer the pan to the oven and bake until the cake springs back when lightly touched in the center with your fingertip and a wooden skewer inserted into the center of the cake comes out clean, about 45 minutes.

6. Remove the pan to a wire rack to cool completely.

7. The cake may be covered tightly and stored at room temperature for up to 2 days. Cut into 12 equal pieces just before serving. If desired, sift a generous amount of powdered sugar over each piece.

VARIATIONS

Fruit-and-Crumb-Topped Coffee Cake *Scatter 4 cups blueberries, pitted cherries, halved apricots or plums, or sliced peaches evenly over the cake batter after scraping it into the pan, then top with the crumb mixture and bake as directed.*

Nut-and-Crumb-Topped Coffee Cake *Add 1 1/2 cups chopped nuts of choice to the crumb topping mixture before sprinkling it over the batter.*

index

95

table of equivalents

The exact equivalents in the following tables have been rounded for convenience.

LIQUID/DRY MEASURES

U.S.	metric
1/4 teaspoon	1.25 milliliters
1/2 teaspoon	2.5 milliliters
1 teaspoon	5 milliliters
1 tablespoon (3 teaspoons)	15 milliliters
1 fluid ounce (2 tablespoons)	30 milliliters
1/4 cup	60 milliliters
1/3 cup	80 milliliters
1/2 cup	120 milliliters
1 cup	240 milliliters
1 pint (2 cups)	480 milliliters
1 quart (4 cups, 32 ounces)	960 milliliters
1 gallon (4 quarts)	3.84 liters
1 ounce (by weight)	28 grams
1 pound	454 grams
2.2 pounds	1 kilogram

LENGTH

U.S.	metric
1/8 inch	3 millimeters
1/4 inch	6 millimeters
1/2 inch	12 millimeters
1 inch	2.5 centimeters

OVEN TEMPERATURE

fahrenheit	celsius	gas
250	120	1/2
275	140	1
300	150	2
325	160	3
350	180	4
375	190	5
400	200	6
425	220	7
450	230	8
475	240	9
500	260	10

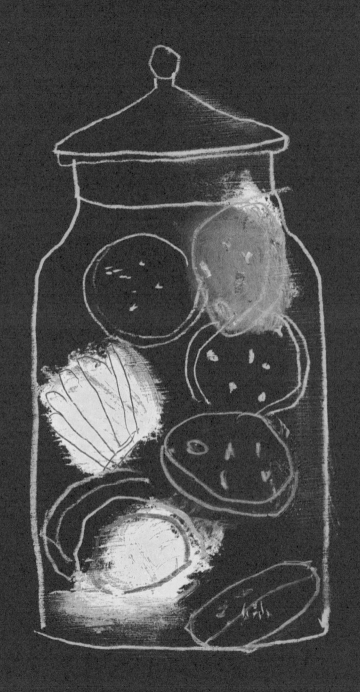